SELF-ESTEEM
Understanding a Complex Phenomenon

A Manual for Mentors

©2010 Lou Thompson. Illustrated by Mal McGill. edited by Dr Graham Lawler

This edition published by Aber Publishing PO Box 225 Abergele, Conwy County LL18 9AY

E-mail: info@aber-publishing.co.uk   Web Site: www.aber-publishing.co.uk

The advice mentioned in this book is given in good faith. The author and the publishers and their agents cannot be held acountable for outcomes related to activities mentioned herein

Aber Publishing is a division of GLMP Ltd

Aber Education

INTRODUCTION

There is a consensus amongst educators that an essential ingredient in the enhancement of youth self-esteem is the quality of the relationship between the child and 'significant others' in his or her life. *(Rogers 1955; Coopersmith 1967; Cotton 1984; Lawrence 1991.)*

The numerous research studies cited by Coopersmith (1975), Yawkey (1980) and Canella (1986) support the claim that 'significant others' can have a positive influence on young people who have unhealthy self-esteem.

Most sources indicate that parents, teachers, peers, community role models and sports coaches, both in primary and secondary schools, influence self-esteem by the feedback they provide about an individual's physical, emotional, social and functional self. Lack of opportunities for youth to have contact with appropriate 'significant others' leaves them open to whatever influences, chance occasions and contacts that are available. This can lead to inappropriate risk taking which in turn can develop into a variety of inappropriate behaviours.

This manual provides a training programme for 'care givers' - teachers, parents, social workers, sports coaches, etc. who wish to maximize their impact as 'significant others' in the process of enhancing children's self-esteem.

The anticipated outcome of this programme is that participating 'care givers' will become effective self-esteem mentors.

CONTENTS

Overview
Essential Self-Esteem Mentor Competencies

To be an effective 'significant other' self-esteem mentors should display as many of the following competencies as possible.

General

1. The self-esteem mentor needs to be able to accept the child as a 'person' even though they may not accept the child's behaviour.

2. The self-esteem mentor needs to be spontaneous and natural when relating with the children.

3. The self-esteem mentor needs to be able to reveal his or her own personality to the children without fear.

4. The self-esteem mentor needs to display empathy to the children. This is the ability to display that they know and feel what it is like to be another person.

5. The self-esteem mentor needs to have a healthy self-esteem themselves.

6. The self-esteem mentor needs to consistently model basic values and standards.

7. The self-esteem mentor is able to establish a trust relationship with children.

Specific

1. The self-esteem mentor needs to display reflective listening skills.

2. The self-esteem mentor needs to display assertive verbal and non-verbal communication skills.

3. The self-esteem mentor needs to display the ability to provide appropriate affirmation.

4. The self-esteem mentor needs to be able to apply appropriate conflict resolution strategies.

5. The self-esteem mentor needs to be able to apply goal setting strategies.

6. The self-esteem mentor needs to be able to demonstrate positive self-talk strategies.

7. The self-esteem mentor needs to be familiar with appropriate relaxation techniques.

8. The self-esteem mentor needs to have an awareness and understanding of basic theoretical concepts related to self-esteem.

9. The self-esteem mentor needs to be familiar with key behaviour indicators of at-risk self-esteem.

10. The self-esteem mentor needs to be familiar with community resources and services that can supplement their endeavours.

Chapter 1
Understanding A Complex Phenomenon
- A Practical Model

SELF-ESTEEM
Understanding A Complex Phenomena
A Practical Model

To maximise their role as 'significant others', self-esteem mentors need to have a sound, pragmatic understanding of the self-esteem phenomenon.

1. Why should we be concerned about youth self-esteem?

There is increasing concern being expressed that the current social and economic pressures that permeate across all sectors of western society are taking a toll on the quality of life styles of increasing numbers of youth. Studies have revealed that significant numbers of youth are reporting problems with depression, anxiety, controlling temper, stress and personal relationships. *(1) (2) (3)*

Care givers understand that a healthy self-esteem is vital to children's well being. A review of the literature points to two key areas in which healthy self-esteem has a positive influence. *(Lawrence 1989; Hendrick, J 1988; Cotton 1984; Coopersmith 1967.)*

1.1 Performance Behaviour

Children with a healthy self-esteem are most likely to utilize their top 10-20% of potential. They freely move out of their performance 'comfort zones' and in doing so are willing to take acceptable risks. By taking these acceptable risks they are prepared to attempt tasks they perceive that they might fail at and, additionally, they are willing to undertake tasks that are entirely new. The performance of a child with healthy self-esteem will not be hindered by an underlying 'fear of failure'.

There are what Professor House website calls 'glaring red flags' that scream out' my self-esteem is low', (http://www.professorshouse.com/family/children/low-self-esteem-in-teenagers.aspx)

1.2 Social Development

Children with a healthy self-esteem are most likely to display confidence in their interpersonal relationships, resolve conflicts positively and communicate assertively. They are able to handle group interactions positively and display appropriate team membership qualities. Above all children with a healthy self-esteem are able to maintain respect for their own **individuality** whilst participating in group or team activities.

They conclude that *'It's OK to be different'*.

---

(1) *Death and hospital admissions from suicide attempts among young people are problems that have grown significantly in the past decade.*
(2) *Surveys of youth self-esteem in Western Australia have revealed that this is an area of concern.*
(3) *The data available collectively suggests that a priority focus for schools and homes should be the enhancement of quality life style amongst youth, in particular, their self-esteem.*
(4) http://www.professorshouse.com/family/children/low-self-esteem-in-teenagers.aspx

2. Clarification of terminology

The literature associated with self-esteem is characterised by a proliferation of often ambiguous terminology. For self-esteem mentors to become effective they need to have a clear understanding of the related terms and concepts. The following definitions and the explanations of terms are offered in the context in which they have been applied to this programme's underlying model and theoretical considerations.

2.1 Self-Concept

This is a generic term that *consists of the beliefs, hypotheses and assumptions that the individual has about himself. It is the person's view of himself as conceived and organised from his inner vantage. The self-concept includes the person's ideas of the kind of person he is, the characteristics that he possesses, and his most important and striking traits.* (Coopersmith and Feldman, 1974, p. 198)

2.2 Self-Esteem

This is the evaluative component of the self-concept and is formed as a result of receiving feedback from the external environment.

☐ *Self-esteem pertains to the evaluation of self-worth which depends on how the culture values the attributes one possesses and how well one's behaviour matches personal standards of worthiness.*
(Bandura, 1986, p. 410)

2.3 The Hattie View

Hattie (1992) takes a somewhat unique tack when attempting to differentiate between self-concept and self-esteem. Hattie's is a cognitive approach which suggests that:

SELF-CONCEPT is merely a set of beliefs and relationships between these beliefs, that we have about ourselves.

SELF-ESTEEM, on the other hand, has to do not only with rational faculties but with commitment and salience.

Hattie contends that:

☐ *It is with respect to our differing perceptions of commitment that we can conceive of self-esteem. Our conceptions of our self-esteem are relative to what we consider important, not necessarily to our capabilities and/or knowledge. (Hattie, 1992, pp. 54, 97)*

2.4 The Lawrence View

It is Lawrence's interpretation of the associated terms that have been drawn upon in the model presented in this programme.

☐ **SELF-CONCEPT** *is an umbrella term because subsumed beneath the 'SELF' there are three aspects:*
SELF-IMAGE (what the person is);
IDEAL SELF (what the person would like to be);
and SELF-ESTEEM (what the person feels about the discrepancy between what he/she is and what he/she would like to be.)
(Lawrence, 1988, p. 2)

3. Theoretical basis for the self-esteem model

The SELF-ESTEEM MODEL which provides the framework for this programme's approach has its theoretical origins in the work done by Katz and Zigler (1967) and Katz, Zigler and Zelk (1975). They claim that children not only build up a concept of themselves - what their own personalities are like and how they are seen by others *(self-image)*, but they also construct a concept of what they would like to be *(ideal image)*. Katz, Zigler and Zelk suggest that a gap between the real, current self *(self-image)* and the ego ideal *(ideal image)* is a sign of maturity.

4. The Self-Esteem Model

For this programme Katz, Zigler and Zelk's theoretical explanations have been translated into the following model.

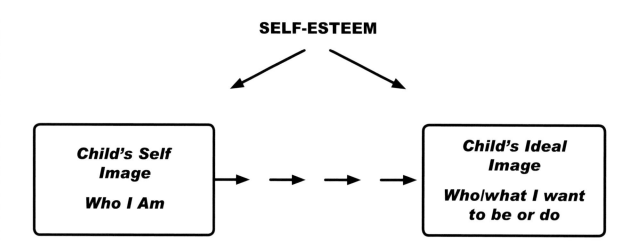

Explanation of Key Components

1. The Self-Image

The **self-image** represents the child's collected thoughts, impressions and knowledge of who he or she is. It includes information related to physical appearance, emotionality, personality, intellectual levels, social roles and functional self *(what I can/cannot do)*.

- ❐ A child's self-image is dynamic, ever changing. New experiences, developmental phenomena and/or changed circumstances will result in the adolescent adding to, modifying or revising their self image. The development of self-image begins from birth as the infant watches the movement of its arms and legs and continues to change and develop as new experiences are encountered throughout life.

- ❐ *... In its practical form (self-image) is personally constructed out of interactions with the environment, in other words, it is learned.*
   (J. A. Beane, 1991.)

2. The Ideal Image

The **ideal image** represents children's collected thoughts, perceptions, ideas and knowledge of who or what they want to be or do ... it represents their goals, dreams and expectations.

- ❐ *Some children's (ideal image) is very similar to their concept of their self-image and they do not aspire to be more than what they believe they already are. For other children the (ideal image) is sometimes a distant goal, something to be worked toward. Sometimes the ideal self is realistic, sometimes it is almost pure fantasy.*
   (J. A. Beane, 1991.)

In any case it is our claim that there is a relationship between children's perception of their SELF-IMAGE and their IDEAL IMAGE. Specifically we would claim that many of children's goals, dreams and expectations are set in place on the basis of their knowledge and perception of who they are.

- ❐ In Workbook 3 we illustrate this claim with the following examples.

Self-Image:	*Ideal Image:*
❐ I did okay at primary school.	❐ I want to do okay at my high school leaving exams.
❐ I am successful with my maths and science.	❐ I want to go to university.
❐ I did well in manual arts, home science.	❐ I want to be able to build, cook, panel-beat, make wine, etc.
❐ I get on well with my friends.	❐ I would like a boyfriend/girlfriend.
❐ I did well with my surfing, cricket, netball, football during primary school.	❐ I want to represent my school, country at surfing, cricket, netball, etc. I want to continue being involved with my sport.

3. The notion of self-esteem within this model

It needs to be recognized that self-esteem is the evaluative component of self-concept. As mentioned earlier:

❐ *Self-esteem pertains to the evaluation of self image which depends on how the culture values the attributes one possesses*
and
how well our behaviour matches personal standards of worthiness. *(Bandura, 1986)*

❐ Our programme argues that the ideal image is a dynamic, motivational force and/or magnet. It is the pursuit of narrowing the gap between **'who I am'** and **'who I want to be or do'** that is the essence of self-esteem.

❐ We claim that it is this association that provides children with the 'motivational force' that encourages them ...

   ❐ to have a go;

   ❐ to take acceptable risks;

   ❐ to use their potential;

   ❐ to cope with mistakes;

   ❐ to stick at tasks until they are completed;

   ❐ to step out of their comfort zones.

❐ We argue that healthy self-esteem does not require every child to totally bridge the gap between their **self-image** and their **ideal image**. Rather they need to feel, at any given time, that they are moving in the right direction towards their goals.

The Key Processes Involved

The development of (self-esteem) involves the overlapping of many factors. It permeates the development of each individual and usually is learned implicitly or indirectly through such factors as empathy, delay of gratification and learning personal control.
(Hattie, 1992 p. 138.)

In this program we have expanded on Hattie's claim and concluded that two key processes are related to the enhancement of positive SELF-ESTEEM.
(See also Book 1, p 9; Book 2, p 10 and Book 3, pp 8-9)

We have identified the two key processes as SELF-DISCOVERY and FEEDBACK FROM SIGNIFICANT OTHERS.

It is in the latter aspect that you, as self-esteem mentors, have a particular role.

❏ Self-Discovery

Children will build their self image and ideal image by having the opportunities to discover as much about their identities as possible.

This requires them to have the opportunity to:

❏ undertake new learning activities;

❏ be involved in problem solving situations;

❏ be involved in activities where 'it's okay to make mistakes' i.e. failure may be viewed as a positive experience;

❏ be involved in situations where they can push themselves to their performance limits;

❏ above all - TO UNDERTAKE CHALLENGE!

The Importance of Challenge

An increasing number of educators are pointing to the importance of CHALLENGE for the enhancement of child self-esteem. Mentors might consider the following thoughts offered by Bandura (1977) and O'Brien (1990).

Bandura (1977) claims that removing a 'fear of failure' requires children to raise their levels of **'expectation of being effective'**. He suggests two sources are important -

PERFORMANCE ACCOMPLISHMENTS

and

VICARIOUS EXPERIENCE

Performance Accomplishments

By this Bandura is suggesting that children, through acquiring levels of mastery, succeed in accomplishing a task. Such successes raise many expectations (and enrich goals and dreams in their ideal image). Through such successes the negative impact of occasional failure is reduced. The reality is, that if through acquired mastery a child meets a challenge, the failures they experience in pursuit of this challenge are positively reflected upon. The notion is, that as a consequence of meeting a specific challenge, children will develop the perception that _occasional failures are okay. They simply strengthen your resolve to persist._

Vicarious Experience

This occurs when children observe others performing challenging activities with no unpleasant consequences.
The usual reaction to this will be ... **_'If they can do it, so can I!'_**
The individual will then intensify his/her efforts to achieve a similar task.

O'Brien (1990) suggests that any programme established to work at enhancing children's self-esteem needs to provide a non-threatening environment so that whatever sense of control they already possess is not immediately eliminated. Any activity/experience that children encounter as part of their self-esteem development needs to encourage them to own their success and develop positive responsibilities for their own behaviour.

Undertaking challenge addresses many of the concerns expressed by Bandura and O'Brien.

❑ Feedback from Significant Others

Children constantly examine their self-image and ideal image via the feedback they receive from significant others in their lives. Lack of opportunities for children to have contact with appropriate 'significant others' leaves them open to whatever influences and chance occasions and contacts that are available.

Studies have indicated that for most children the following people represent the significant others they need access to:

- ❑ mum/dad and family members (brothers, sisters, grandmothers, grandfathers, etc.);

- ❑ teachers;

- ❑ the peer group;

- ❑ community role models (sports coaches, sporting celebrities, media-entertainment celebrities, high profile community service personnel, etc.).

The order of choice of significant other will fluctuate according to what aspect of 'self' is being reviewed. Most importantly, children need to feel confident that all sources of feedback are accessible if they need them.

This last point is particularly important for adolescents when you consider the following claim by Erikson.

Erikson suggests that most adolescents enter a period of MORATORIUM in which they try out many roles and personalities before making hard and fast decisions (about their _ideal image_).

It is therefore vital that the opportunity is available for students to take part in challenging situations in which they receive feedback from a variety of valued persons whom they see as contributing, successful members of society.

'At Risk' Self-Esteem

The Self-Esteem Wall

Underlying a child's low self-esteem is a 'fear of failure'. This 'fear of failure' is not always readily apparent to parents or teachers, nor based upon an adolescent's realistic evaluation of his/her current performance levels.

For some children this inappropriate 'fear of failure' has its origins in a distorted or incomplete self-image. For reasons that are sometimes obscure they conclude:

I am different from others. This is unacceptable to others.
I don't like my individual self. It is inevitable that I will fail.
I wish I could change who I am.

For children who have low self-esteem because of an inappropriate self-image, intervention needs to be directed at building up their awareness and acceptance of their individual self.

For the majority of children who have an inappropriate 'fear of failure' the key source for the dilemma is related to an inappropriate ideal image.

If a child reaches the stage where he or she conclude:

❐ I cannot meet the expectations that are part of my ideal image;

❐ I will not achieve the goals that are part of my ideal image;

❐ the dreams and aspirations that are part of my ideal image are meaningless;

❐ they are likely to hit the **SELF-ESTEEM WALL**.

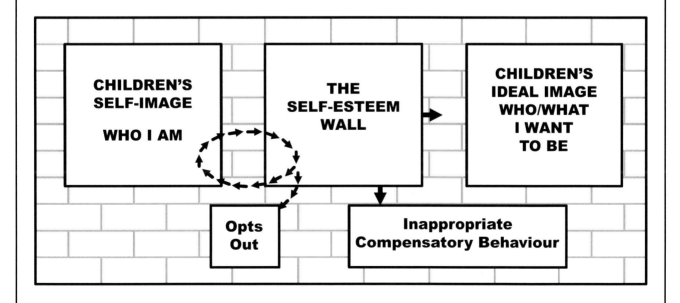

A Special Concern Regarding Adolescent Ideal Image

❑ During adolescence increasing emphasis is placed on the ideal of *'getting a good job!'* Many adolescents conclude that if they are going to be valued by parents/society the securing of a 'good job', however they might define this, is paramount. Gradually many of the 'non-work' ideals (recreational, cultural, social) are devalued and replaced by a very narrowly perceived work ethic ideal.

In current economic times of high youth unemployment this can be a recipe for disastrous self-esteem consequences. Significant numbers of adolescents come to a conclusion:

I am not going to get the 'good job' everyone says I should get;

I'm not going to get into University/College;

I have no chance of getting a job.

... they then hit the **SELF-ESTEEM WALL!**

Parents and teachers need to encourage adolescents to maintain and value *NON-WORK IDEALS* whilst they pursue their work-ethic related ideals.

Chapter 2
Children With Special Self-Esteem Needs...
Identifying and Assisting Them

Identification of Children With Special Self-Esteem Needs

❏ Measures of Self-Concept

(Hattie, 1992 pp 140-175)

There seem to be as many measures of self-concept as there are researchers on the topic. Three tests have emerged as more popular than any others:

- The Piers Harris Test (1964)
- The Coopersmith Test (1959)
- The Song Hattie Test (1988).

It is apparent that there is truth in Hattie's claim that the status of testing has dramatically improved over the past 15 years. It is also evident that although estimates of reliability are typically very high, there is still a problem with VALIDITY of the test being used.

Although we recognize the importance of the measures mentioned above we suggest that an effective SELF-ESTEEM MENTOR is in a position to observe particular behaviours that indicate a child has special needs related to the state of their self-esteem.

Our experience suggests that the following behaviours could be telling parents, teachers or mentors the message that a child is experiencing self-esteem difficulties:
(see also Book 1 pp 10 - 11; Book 2 p 13; Book 3 p 12.)

❏ A sudden change in their performance behaviour

This is often reflected in a fall-off in the quantity of their responses. They write less, do fewer maths problems, complete fewer assignments, spend less time studying than has normally been the case. This fall-off in quantity is soon followed by a deterioration of the quality of their responses. An onset of careless errors, untidy work and disorganised responses become unexpectedly commonplace.

❏ A change in their social interactions

This often begins with a sudden change in their social interactions with their brothers and sisters. They attempt to distance themselves from their siblings, wanting nothing to do with them. Sometimes this flows over to their interactions with mum and dad, grandma or grandad. At school, teachers will observe the child increasingly opting out of group interactions with peers and distancing themselves from team sporting situations. Parents will note a dramatic drop off in social phone calls and diminishing home visits by friends.

❏ A change in communication patterns

Many children who are at the self-esteem wall display an onset of aggressive communication, put down statements, pushing away language or no communication at all. This is often first directed at siblings and mum and dad and then flows over into the school situation and is directed at the child's peers and sometimes even the teacher.

❏ Change in emotions

Occasionally children who are at the self-esteem wall show their frustrations and anxieties by displaying inappropriate emotional behaviour. This can include temper-tantrums, mood swings, constant sullenness and/or inappropriate crying.

Aber Education

❑ Obsessional type behaviours

Children who are at the self-esteem wall, as a consequence of their concluding that they are not able to reach social goals such as being accepted by their peer group or attracting a girl/boy friend, sometimes perceive that this is because of their physical appearance. When this is the case, such children may display obsessive dietary behaviour (food deprivation, food excessiveness) or obsessive fitness behaviour (inappropriate jogging, inappropriate lifting of weights, inappropriate aerobics, etc.).

❑ Inappropriate risk taking

Children who conclude that they are not going to achieve other expectations will occasionally embark upon a series of inappropriate risk taking behaviours. These could include truancy, substance abuse, reckless driving.

❑ Inappropriate sleep

Children who might be at the self-esteem wall often have little time during their busy day to reflect on this situation whilst at school or immediately after school. For many the real anxieties, frustrations and uncertainties surface when they retire to bed. Such anxiety based reflection can interfere with their required healthy sleep. A consequence can be that they awake lethargic and not fully revitalised.

In considering the above indicators teachers and carers must exercise caution:

- ❑ A single indicator could be part of the child's normal coping behaviours. Parents and teachers should look for a combination of the above factors.

- ❑ Short episodes of the above behaviours does not necessarily indicate a problem. If a child is at the self-esteem wall they are likely to display the behaviours over a significant period of time.

❑ Assisting Children Climb The Self-Esteem Wall
(See also Book 1 p12-13; Book 2 p14; Book 3 pp13-14.)

The programme outlined in this manual is particularly focused at training self-esteem mentors to become effective in helping children climb the self-esteem wall. We suggest that there are three priorities for self-esteem mentors in their endeavours to assist with this task.

- ❑ Establishing an appropriate relationship.

- ❑ Assisting the child to review, and in some cases, reset their self and ideal images.

- ❑ Providing guidance and strategies the child can utilize in strengthening their resolve in the pursuit of their ideals.

❑ Desirable Qualities In The Self-Esteem Mentor Conducive To Self-Esteem Enhancement *(See also Book 3 p14)*

Studies have indicated that effective self-esteem mentors appear to have particular qualities in themselves. Rogers (1955) has referred to this quality as the ability to feel and project unconditional positive regard. This kind of fundamental acceptance and approval of the child is not contingent upon his/her meeting the mentor's expectations of what he should be, but simply depends on his/her being alive; being a child; being in the group.

We would contend the following qualities are desirable if a mentor is to establish the optimum relationship:

❐ Acceptance

This means the ability to accept the child even though you may not accept the child's behaviour.

> **Ask yourself ...**
> ... am I taking time to enjoy the children or am I looking at them with a critical eye - noting mainly what behaviour should be improved?

If you find you are habitually noting only what should be changed this is a sign that you are losing sight of the importance of appreciating the children as they are right now, no strings attached.

The ability to display acceptance implies a faith in the way the child will turn out, an attitude that subtly makes him or her aware that the mentor has confidence he or she will grow in sound directions. There is no substitute for these underlying feelings of trust and confidence in the child.

Acceptance of the child as he or she is also includes accepting his or her right to be different from the mentor and from other children.

❐ Honest Recognition and Praise

To be an effective esteem raiser, givers of praise should include information about something specific a child has achieved. *(Cannella, 1986)*

We need to be careful not to dole out praise in such a mechanical way that it comes to have almost no meaning at all.

Using encouragement rather than praise is another effective way of building self-esteem. Comments such as ...

... Look how much work you have done!

... Good on you - a great try!

encourage children without passing judgement on what they've done.

Children need to learn that failing at something is not the end of the world. For this reason it is also important to appreciate the effort of children when they have not been successful.

❐ Respect

One basic way to show respect is to abide by the child's decision when he or she has been given a valid choice.

Children also feel respected when a mentor asks their opinion and listens carefully to their replies.

A mentor shows respect of the child by avoiding humiliating him or her in front of other people.

Coopersmith (1967), who carried out an extensive study of children possessing high self-esteem, found that parents of such youngsters were firm in their control of them, but also took time to explain the reasons for their actions. Such reasoning confers respect because it assumes that the child is important enough to be entitled to an explanation and intelligent enough to comprehend it.

Chapter 3
The Importance of Mentors' Self-Esteem

The Importance of Mentors' Self-Esteem

3.1   General

There is well documented evidence pointing to the relationship between the possession of positive self-esteem and the possession of positive attitudes to others (Lawrence, 1988; Burns, 1975). The possession of positive self-esteem facilitates the construction of warm, supportive relations with others.

We cannot easily value other people without first valuing ourselves. Lawrence (1988) claims that children who 'model' themselves on 'significant others' with high self-esteem will be enthusiastic and confident and their communication with other children will be easy and relaxed. Low self-esteem in significant others results in a feeling of inadequacy being communicated. Children learn to feel defensive and insecure.

This programme presents prospective SELF-ESTEEM MENTORS with strategies which can be utilized to enhance their own self-esteem.

These strategies, which are described in detail on the following pages, include:

1.   Taking time out for self-assessment.

2.   Reviewing your access to 'significant other' sources.

3.   Reviewing your personal objectives and aspirations.

4.   Developing your verbal/non-verbal communication skills.

5.   Identifying potential sources of stress and familiarizing yourself with effective stress-management strategies.

6.   Identifying relevant relaxation techniques for yourself. Taking regular physical exercise.

3.2   Taking time out for self-assessment

In our work we refer to the importance of a healthy **self-image**. The work includes a number of activities designed to enhance children's **self-image**. What follows are a number of considerations for potential self-esteem mentors to reflect on in terms of their own **self-image**.

If a self-esteem mentor is to display acceptance, genuineness, and empathy to the children they are working with it is crucial that they have a detailed self-awareness. A basic premise underlying healthy self-esteem is:

❏ *that belief in self is dependent upon knowledge of self.*

Because they are 'caring', community conscious, conscientious, responsible people there is a danger for potential self-esteem mentors, that over a significant period of time, they devote great energies in trying to be the person they think others want them to be.

    ... The perfect parent.

    ... The perfect teacher.

    ... The perfect social worker, etc.

This is **not** conducive to the possession of a healthy self-esteem. The outcome can be that they have lost sight of their **real** 'warts and all' self. It is often the case that people who are not fully familiar with their real self underestimate their potential.

❏ Self-respect is built upon self-awareness. If you don't respect yourself how can you expect other people to respect you? Self-awareness leads to self-trust. Self-trust is essential to a healthy self-esteem.

The following suggestions/activities are designed to assist potential self-esteem mentors become more familiar with their REAL SELF.

3.21 Carrying Out a Self-Assessment

In carrying out a self-assessment you might give some consideration to the following suggestions.

❏   Keep a Diary

Often an on-going written, personal record reveals aspects of self more spontaneously, honestly and directly than any other means. In keeping such a diary the following lead in phrases can often stimulate key information about your real self:

    ❏ Today I feel ...

    ❏ Today I did ...

    ❏ Today I was proud of the way I ...

    ❏ Today I didn't handle ...

    ❏ Today I enjoyed the company of ...

    ❏ Today I was angry with the following behaviour shown by ...

    ❏ Today my mood was dominated by feelings of ...

    ❏ Today I was disappointed with ...

❏ Find Your Personal Space

We live in a hurly burly, ever changing, always demanding world. Often we conclude *'I don't have time to think!'*

To honestly reflect on self we need access to a non-threatening, familiar, comfortable, private location, i.e. you need to find your personal space.

In this situation there is less likelihood of interfering variables to disrupt our reflections.

FINDING YOUR PERSONAL SPACE

❏   *Reflection on the following questions will help you identify your personal space:*

Which piece of music makes you most at peace, relaxed?

Answer ....

Which is your favourite/most comfortable chair at home?

Answer ....

Which is the part of your home in which you most enjoy being?

Answer ....

Do you have a favourite animal whose company makes you feel good?

Answer ....

Do you have a favourite walk?

Answer ....

Is their a particular 'vista' you have access to that you find relaxing?

Answer ....

Do you have a leisure activity that you can engage in that takes your mind away from the stresses of normal living?

Answer ....

Is there a time of day when you feel most relaxed?

Answer ....

Do you have a favourite passage of prose or a poem that you find inspirational or relaxing?

Answer ....

Is there a painting that, when you view it, has an uplifting effect on you?

Answer ....

The suggestion is that if you can place yourself in any combination of the above situations you will be in a SPACE that will allow you to appropriately REFLECT ON YOUR SELF-IMAGE.

Aber Education

❏ Take 'Time Out' to Conduct a Self-Awareness Inventory

This is best conducted in your personal space.

Simply reflect on the questions posed ... even if it's just in your own mind.

The notion behind this activity is to alert you to how well (or otherwise) you know your real self. Take particular note of those questions you are unable to answer ... then make a commitment to finding the missing information.

MY PHYSICAL SELF

What is my blood pressure?...

What is my cholesterol reading? ....

What is my weight? ....

What is my height?...

How fit am I? ....

What parts of my body am I proud, comfortable, positive about?.............................

....

What parts of my body have changed in recent times? ....

What parts of my body cause me anxiety? ....

What parts of my body would I like more information about? ....

    The status of my heart?...................................

    The quality of my eyesight?...................................

    The quality of my hearing? ....

What parts of my body would I like to change?...................................

....

MY EMOTIONAL SELF

What makes me angry? ....

What behaviours do I display when I'm angry? ....

Can I control my anger? ....

What do I fear? ....

How do these fears affect my behaviour? ....

What makes me happy? ....

How do I behave when I'm happy? ....

What makes me depressed? ....

What gives me 'peace of mind'? ....

Do I ever display temper tantrums? ....

    When? ....

    Why? ....

What causes me to stress? ....

Do I feel loved? ....

Do I show love? ....

How do I display love? ....

Do I experience jealousy? What? Who? makes me feel jealous? ....

....

What aspects of my Emotional Self would I like to change? ....

MY ATTITUDES/VALUES

What standards are important to my daily living? ....

....

What are my current religious/political beliefs? ....

What life qualities are important to me? ....

....

Which 'role models' impress me? ....

Are there any attitudes or values that I currently have that I would like to change?

....

....

MY SOCIAL SELF

Do I make friends easily? ....

Can I speak in front of others comfortably? ....

Do I have some 'SOUL' friends? ....

Am I happy to be part of a team? ....

Do I prefer to be on my own? ....

Am I an 'outgoing' extroverted person? ....

or

Am I a quiet introverted person? ....

Could I be a leader? ....

MY FUNCTIONAL SELF

What did I do well today? ....

What significant tasks did I complete recently? ....

Who have I helped recently? ....

Over the last few weeks/months what have been my most significant achievements?

....

Have I surprised myself with any recent achievements? ....

What failures have I recently had? ....

What things could I have done better? ....

....

Why don't you record in your personal diaries any responses that you have given that either ...

❑ fill you with pride;

❑ cause you some personal concern?

3.3 **To maintain healthy self-esteem a mentor should take time to review the identity of, and their access to, 'significant other' sources.**

Whilst a parent, teacher, social worker, sports coach, etc. readily accepts that they are a 'significant other' to the children for whom they are responsible, they often take for granted, underestimate or are just simply unaware of, those people in their own lives who are their 'significant others'. To have a healthy self-esteem, mentors too need access to people who will provide them with trusted feedback.

It is a productive and sometimes revealing exercise for prospective mentors to take time out to review this vital component of their self-esteem.

A useful exercise is for the prospective mentor to record their responses to the following checklist:

SIGNIFICANT OTHER CHECKLIST

☐ At this point of time who would I be able to talk to about personal matters?

Ans ....

☐ Within my family (immediate family, extended family) whose opinions do I respect?

Ans ....

☐ Outside of my family whose opinions do I respect regarding ...

my physical appearance	Ans ....
my emotional self	Ans ....
my social self	Ans ....
my functional self	Ans ....

☐ At my place of employment whose performance do I respect?

Ans ....

☐ At my place of employment whose advice/feedback do I most respect?

Ans ....

☐ In the world at large which people stand out for me as:

☆ high achievers	Ans ....
☆ good role models	Ans ....
☆ good parents	Ans ....
☆ good citizens	Ans ....

3.4   Reviewing Your Personal Objectives and Aspirations

We have, in our work, emphasized the importance of the ability to set realistic goals for the development of a healthy ideal image.

Stephen Covey is a world leader in thinking on this area and we highly recommend his best selling books *The 7 Habits of Highly Successful People, Principle Centred Leadership and First Things First.*

A PROSPECTIVE SELF-ESTEEM MENTOR NEEDS TO CONSTANTLY REVIEW AND SET PERSONAL OBJECTIVES.

How long ago was it that you sat down and reflected on your ...

   life focus?

   short and long term goals?

   dreams and aspirations?

   The activity on the following page will assist you in reviewing your goals.

GOAL SETTING ACTIVITY

☐ Step One

Take time to reflect on your current lifestyle. After a short time ask yourself:

Are there any aspects of my lifestyle that I would like to:

change? Ans. ....

☐ improve? Ans. ....

☐ increase, develop further? Ans. ....

☐ maintain, continue in just the same way? Ans. ....

....

☐ Step Two

Select 1 or 2 (no more than 3) of your responses and write them down according to the following format:

In the next few days **(short-term goal)** I would like to (change or improve or increase

or maintain) ... .

....

In the next few weeks, months, year **(long-term goal)** I would like to (change or

improve or increase or maintain) ....

....

In the next few years, decade **(dream)** I would like to (change or improve or increase

or maintain) ... .

....

☐ Step Three

Select, and then add to your goal statements, suitable criterion that will provide you with an indication as to how close to your goal you have moved.

e.g. **Goal Statement**

In the next few weeks I would like to increase the time I spend with my son.

Criteria
I will spend 30 minutes between 6 pm and 8 pm Tuesday, Wednesday and Thursday evenings exclusively with my son.

☐ Step Four

Write your goal statement/s into your personal diary.

3.5   There is a relationship between healthy self-esteem and healthy communication.

Self-esteem mentors should be aware that the manner in which they communicate provides information to others about how they feel about themselves.

A person who has confidence in his or her communication style and skills will communicate more honestly, more positively and more assertively with others.

It is suggested that the more self-esteem mentors are aware of their communication 'self', the more they will be able to empathize with their children and the more purposefully they will communicate with them.

The following activities are designed to assist self-esteem mentors to further develop their communication self-awareness:

HOW GOOD ARE YOUR LISTENING SKILLS?

For this activity mentors should work in pairs. The 'CHECKLIST' referred to can be found on the next page.

- ☐ Mentor 1 relates to Mentor 2 any emotional event in his or her life (a new job - a family mishap - a sporting/work/study failure - a special holiday). The talk should be approximately 5 minutes in duration.

- ☐ Immediately after their discourse Mentor 1 should complete the associated checklist.

- ☐ Roles are then reversed with Mentor 2 relating an emotional event to Mentor 1.

- ☐ After Mentor 2 has completed the checklist the mentors separately comment on each other's listening behaviour using the checklist responses as their guide.

LISTENING BEHAVIOUR CHECKLIST

☐ Did you feel you were being understood?

.................Yes, a great deal   ....Mostly   ....Not at all

☐ Did the listener maintain appropriate eye contact?

.................Yes   ....Occasionally   ....Not at all

☐ Did the listener reflect your feelings?

.................Yes   ....Occasionally   ....Not at all

☐ Did the listener do too much talking?

.................Yes   ....Occasionally   ....Not at all

☐ Did you feel you were being supported by the listener?

.................Yes   ....Occasionally   ....Not at all

☐ Did the listener make you feel you were in an inferior role?

.................Yes   ....Occasionally   ....Not at all

☐ Were you distracted in any way by the listener?

.................Yes   ....Occasionally   ....Not at all

☐ Did the listener help you to feel at ease?

.................Yes   ....Occasionally   ....Not at all

HOW POSITIVE IS YOUR NON-VERBAL COMMUNICATION?

For this activity mentors should work as a threesome.

Mentors 1 and 2 enter into a debate on a controversial topic: (e.g. Legal Abortion, Euthanasia, Decriminalizing Marijuana Smoking etc.).

Each mentor is to take a stand on the issue. The debate should last for approximately 5 minutes.

Mentor 3 acts as the observer and ranks Mentor 1 and 2 on non-verbal behaviour according to the associated checklist. He/she then provides Mentors 1 and 2 feedback about their non-verbal communication performance.

Participants rotate so that Mentor 3 can also be rated.

NON-VERBAL COMMUNICATION CHECKLIST

Did the participant display ...	Yes	No
☐ **Facial Expressions?**		
Smile	....	....
Frown	....	....
Grimace	....	....
☐ **Hand Gestures?**		
Point	....	....
Touch	....	....
Wave	....	....
Fidget	....	....
Fold Arms	....	....
Put hands in pockets	....	....
☐ **Eye Contact?**		
Avoid eye contact	....	....
Stare	....	....
Flit from position to position	....	....
☐ **Body Orientation?**		
Stand too close	....	....
Continuously move	....	....
Stand too far away	....	....
Turn away from respondent	....	....
☐ **Tone of Voice?**		
Talk harshly	....	....
Talk too softly	....	....
Talk too loudly	....	....
Talk encouragingly	....	....
Talk expressively	....	....
Talk aggressively	....	....

3.6   Stress and Self-Esteem

KEY INFORMATION AND MANAGEMENT STRATEGIES FOR POTENTIAL SELF-ESTEEM MENTORS

❏ *Stress is the physiological and psychological reaction which occurs when a person's perceived capacity is insufficient to meet the demands of a situation. Stress is a non specific response by the body to demands made upon it.*
(Seyle, 1956)

Given the all encompassing nature of unhealthy stress, it can have a long-term negative effect on a person's self-esteem. It is recognised that unhealthy stress can cause:

❏ extreme fatigue, exhaustion, continual overwork;

❏ loss of enthusiasm, energy, drive;

❏ feelings of depersonalization towards clients; defensiveness;

❏ loss of imagination and creativity;

❏ reluctance to change; inflexibility;

❏ poor memory; disorganization;

❏ sarcasm;

❏ withdrawal.
(Pines and Aronson, 1980)

These stress outcomes can have a significant negative influence on one's **SELF-IMAGE** and **IDEAL-IMAGE**.

It is our contention that to be an effective self-esteem mentor one needs to:

❏ understand some of the basic concepts and facts related to stress;

❏ be familiar with potential stressors;

❏ have access to key stress management strategies.

In this programme we would like to provide some guidance, information and focus on the following related topics:

❏ Some Key Facts Related To Stress

❏ The Issue of 'Burn Out' and Potential Stressors

❏ General Management Strategies

Aber Education

3.61 Key Facts, Concepts Related To Stress
(Understanding Your Own Stress)

Stressors arise from two main sources:

Physical Conditions that have the potential to damage the body (e.g. starvation, accident, hypothermia).

Psychological Situations (e.g. intense persistent fears or prolonged, unresolved conflict).

An event or situation that constitutes a stressor to one person (e.g. fear of exams) will not necessarily be a stressor for another person.

It is generally accepted that the primary stress response produces a common pattern of physiological reactions. These have been identified as follows:

- An increase in heart rate and blood pressure as blood is forced to those muscle groups which may have to respond immediately to the physical threat imposed.

- Sweating, which is the way the body lowers its temperature, allowing more energy to be utilized.

- Tension throughout the body muscles in preparation for immediate response to the crisis.

- The release of glucose into the bloodstream from the liver. This response provides muscle groups with a readily available source of energy.

- Shallow breathing when the diaphragm tenses. This can lead to a reduced amount of oxygen entering the brain.

Seyle (1956) claims that the body reacts to stress in 3 successive stages:

An alarm reaction
Whenever the body is confronted with a stressor an ALARM REACTION takes place. This consists of a complicated pattern of physiological and chemical changes. One component of this general reaction is the hypothalamic stimulation of the pituitary gland. This gland releases various hormones, one of which stimulates the adrenal cortex to secrete cortin. This hormone helps the body to cope with the impact of a variety of stressors.

The stage of resistance
During this stage the body reactions to stress increase. This often has the effect, especially in non-critical situations, of eliminating the source of stress. However, when the stress situation persists the body's reaction can then become too intense. For example, cortin may be secreted at such a high rate that its supply becomes depleted.

The stage of exhaustion
This occurs when the body depletes the necessary resources to deal with the stressor. Usually the stress has ended before this stage is reached. In those situations when the stage of exhaustion is reached, the consequences can be disastrous, occasionally resulting in death.

Not all stress is bad for you. In fact, without a degree of stress, it is unlikely that you will actualize your potential. An optimum level of stress can motivate you to face challenges with vigour and enthusiasm.

Identifying Stressors and
The Symptoms of Stress

☐ Form a small group of 3 to 5 people. Appoint one person as the recorder.

☐ On a sheet of paper (or below) each individual lists circumstances, events and situations that cause them stress.

....

....

....

....

....

....

☐ The recorder lists responses under two headings:

Individual Responses (Cited by 1 group member only.)	**Common Responses** (Cited by more than 1 group member.)
....	....
....	....
....	....
....	....
....	....

☐ Groups come together and the above exercise is repeated but group recorders report common responses only.

Individual Responses (Cited by 1 group only.)	**Common Responses** (Cited by more than 1 group.)
....	....
....	....
....	....
....	....
....	....

☐ A discussion can follow based on what can be done to manage stress situations.

3.62   Managing Stress: (General Considerations)

There are essentially two considerations:

☐   Stress can work against you.

☐   Stress can work for you.

The important thing is to recognise that we need to manage our stress levels, rather than try to eliminate stress altogether by pretending that the situations which are potentially stressful do not exist and don't need to be faced.

WE NEED TO BE RATIONAL ABOUT STRESS.

The following general management strategies are offered for potential mentors.

Note the **TIMES** or **CIRCUMSTANCES** when you experience unpleasant stress.
☐   Is there a pattern to these experiences?
☐   Are they caused by similar people of stressors?

NOW:

Are there ways to tackle the above situations?

☐   Can you remove or reduce the stressor?

☐   Can you modify your reaction or attitude toward the stressor?

☐   In your personal diary regularly monitor your reaction towards on-going stressors.

☐   Eat healthily, slowly and thoughtfully.

☐   Improve your relationships with people, talking less and listening more.

☐   Make humour and affection part of your daily routine: smile and laugh more and worry less.

☐   Learn patience: walk, don't run; allow yourself time for positive, creative thinking.

☐   Use positive "self-talk" saying

   "I can ..."

   "I will ..."

☐   Wear comfortable clothes and shoes. Change into relaxing clothes when you get home from work.

☐   Accept what cannot be changed and control what can.

☐   Improve your physical health and well being through exercise, yoga, deep breathing, rest and relaxation.

Chapter 4
The Importance of Quality Leisure and Time Management

The Importance of Quality Leisure

In all our accompanying books we have endeavoured to stress the importance of children having a balance between academic achievements and leisure pursuits in their goals, aspirations and dreams. We contend that to have an ideal image totally dominated by academic/work ethic ideals can be very stressful and limiting.

This consideration is equally important to potential self-esteem mentors.

Quality leisure can provide 'breathing space', 'personal space', or an appropriate time to come to terms with the anxieties and fears normally associated with potential stressors.

Often potential self-esteem mentors, because of their conscientious, responsible, care-giving attitudes, put all their 'ideal image' eggs into one basket ... to be the consummate 'significant other'.

This frequently results in their sacrificing their own **quality leisure.**

Our observations have identified the phenomena of **guilt leisure** amongst many care givers ... especially teachers, parents and social workers.

We would explain this phenomena in the following manner:

PARENT:

To be a responsible parent when I'm home I must carry out my domestic responsibilities diligently. I must spend significant time with my children, playing with them, helping them with their homework, taking them to their sport etc. I do not have time to play golf or read my novel ... If I do I feels as though I am neglecting my parental responsibilities.

TEACHER:

My job places many demands and expectations on me. If I'm going to get ahead, earn promotion, then I must meet the requirements. I don't have time for my leisure and when I do engage in my golf the overriding thought going through my mind is: 'I shouldn't be here. I should be home completing my unfinished marking, or preparing work for my next week, or working at my extra university studies.'

This thinking is not healthy. It creates rather than reduces stress.

Give some thought to the following activities:

Construct Your Own Quality Leisure Profile

I am someone who really enjoys ...

EXAMPLES	PRIORITY
walking along the beach	3
playing with my children	2
listening to Mozart	4
painting/potting/sketching	1
dabbling in my garden	5
walking	7
fishing	6

Cross out any reference to your domestic chores or normal work requirements.

Now prioritize your leisure inventory - 1 for the most enjoyable, 2 for the next most enjoyable and so on.

The claim is that when you are engaged in a high priority leisure activity you are in a relative stress free zone. It can be the equivalent of your personal space and allows you to recuperate from the anxieties exerted by work related stressors.

HOWEVER ...

Simply having an inventory of stressors is no guarantee that you will actually build quality leisure engagements into your self-esteem, especially your ideal image. Unless you place some value on your leisure pursuits, they will lie dormant and have little impact on your stress management.

The following activity will give you some insight into your current valuation of your leisure pursuits.

LEISURE ATTITUDE SCALE

Instructions:

This 'self quiz' assesses your leisure attitudes. Make your agreement or disagreement with each of the items below.

	Agree	Disagree
1. I hate to waste time.	☐	☐
2. I normally have more fun at work than on evenings and weekends.	☐	☐
3. I usually take work with me on holiday.	☐	☐
4. I become unusually impatient in traffic jams and while queuing up.	☐	☐
5. I really do not need as many breaks from work as other people seem to need.	☐	☐
6. I enjoy playing games to win.	☐	☐
7. I move, speak, eat and walk rapidly.	☐	☐
8. I'm not as conscious as the average person of beautiful or ugly surroundings. Instead, I focus on the task at hand.	☐	☐
9. I don't really like sightseeing. I'm bored with travel unless I have a concrete purpose for going somewhere.	☐	☐
10. When I'm unable to work I feel guilty.	☐	☐

Items for this questionnaire are original. They are based on ideas found in the following reference sources: Friedman and Roseman (1974), Didator (cited in Hall and Hall, 1979, p. 185).

Scoring:

The more items you agree with, the more anti-leisure you attitudes are . A score of 8 or more agreements suggests that a 'leisure phobia' may be limiting your chances of achieving optimal health and psychological development.

Aber Education

INAPPROPRIATE TIME MANAGEMENT

Inappropriate time management - destroyer of healthy self-esteem; enemy of quality leisure.

"I never have enough time. I always run out of time.
There are just not enough hours in the day.
Time slips through my fingers."

Poor time management creates anxiety, increases stress, interferes with quality leisure pursuits and ultimately can have a negative influence on self-esteem.

Utilizing time more effectively might require potential self-esteem mentors to make changes in their personal work habits; habits which are usually both ingrained and comfortable. Most people waste time because it is satisfying to do so.

TIME MANAGEMENT IS FIRST AND FOREMOST SELF-DISCIPLINE. THERE ARE NOT EASY STRATEGIES FOR GETTING AROUND THIS FACT.

Consider the inventory of time wasters on the following page. Tick the box that reflects your normal response. An analysis of your response might give you some clues about habits that need to be addressed.

INVENTORY OF TIME WASTERS

TIME WASTER	RESPONSE	
	Yes	No
PROCRASTINATION: Putting off necessary tasks, usually because they are unpleasant or boring.	☐	☐
LACK OF PRIORITIES: Doing things on a first come basis without any attempt to discriminate between the importance of tasks.	☐	☐
TELEPHONE INTERRUPTIONS: The phone controls you ... you don't control it.	☐	☐
ATTEMPTING TOO MUCH AT ONE TIME: Tackling several tasks at one time, resulting in no follow-through.	☐	☐
SOCIALIZING: Engaging in frequent chit-chat and personal discussions whilst on the job.	☐	☐
OVERINDULGENCE IN SOCIAL NICETIES: Too many 'long lunches', dinners, extra-long morning/ afternoon teas, etc. Little regard to the importance of the social event to the task at hand.	☐	☐
FAILURE TO LISTEN TO INSTRUCTIONS: This inevitably necessitates you having to go back and remedy things later.	☐	☐
FAILURE TO GIVE CLEAR INSTRUCTIONS: Can be a significant time waster requiring you to repeat them over.	☐	☐
INABILITY TO SAY 'NO': To say "YES" to everyone inevitably means you will take on more than you can cope with, resulting in significant time wastage.	☐	☐
MAIL: There is always the temptation to read it when other tasks have a higher priority.	☐	☐
GETTING COFFEE: Why not take a thermos? To get a cup of coffee can be an excuse to back away from a difficult task.	☐	☐
MEETINGS: 'Meetings, bloody meetings.' Why not prioritize meetings. Learn to say "No" to some. Make sure those that you do attend are efficiently run.	☐	☐

TIME WASTER SELF-AUDIT

A constant emphasis in our approach to self-esteem enhancement, for both youth and potential self-esteem mentors, is the importance of self-awareness.

Let us pose the question - *"How aware are you of your time wastage?"*

Address this by attempting the following activity.

Instructions:

The following 'Log Sheet' should be maintained over two days. It should be attempted by parents in the context of 'domestic employment', or people at their normal place of work.

- ☐ Everything should be recorded, including

    phone calls

    coffee breaks

    unplanned activities.

- ☐ Unless the log is very detailed the data will not be helpful.

- ☐ You need to keep the Log Sheet in a place where activities can be logged as they occur.

- ☐ Just keeping the Log Sheet demands self discipline.

- ☐ A different Log Sheet should be used for each day.

TIME WASTER SELF AUDIT
LOG SHEET

TIME			DATE ...../...../.....
FROM	TO	MINUTES	DESCRIPTION OF ACTIVITY

ANALYSING YOUR TIME WASTER SELF-AUDIT

Showing diligence in analysing your **self-audit** is an important step towards developing the **discipline** referred to previously.

To this end we have provided you with a **Self-Analysis Sheet**. (next page)

A different Self-Analysis Sheet should be used for each day of your Log.

In analysing the Log, it is important to focus on how personal enquiries are being digested.

Ask yourself ...

☐ Are things that consume most of my time really important in terms of my goals, dreams and aspirations?

☐ What consumes my time that I dislike?

☐ What consumes my time that I really enjoy?

Now ...

Determine how much discretionary time you really have.

Look at your leisure time priorities.

Which ones can you now select and use?

Work on the basis most people have only one and a half hours of 'own time' a day.

We would contend ...

That all potential self-esteem mentors can increase their **'own time'** by over two hours by energetically working at getting rid of unnecessary time wasters.

If you are going to be an effective self-esteem mentor, above all else you must focus on effectively utilizing your 1.5 - 2.5 hours of discretionary time available.

Be selective. Set and observe daily priorities.

TIME WASTER LONG ANALYSIS SHEET

DATE ...../...../.....

After completing your time waster self audit, review the results and answer the following questions:

☐ What goals did you set for today?

☐ What goals did you accomplish?

☐ What goals did you make progress towards?

☐ **Interruptions**

What was the longest time you spent without interruptions? ....

How many interruptions did you have today? ....

Who was the most frequent interrupter during the day? ....

☐ **Inappropriate social interruptions/indulgences:**

How much time did you spend in social chit-chat?...

How many coffees did you have? ....

How many personal telephone calls did you participate in? ....

How long was your lunch break? ....

How many times did you phone your family?..

☐ **What was the most productive part of your day?**

....

☐ **What things did you do today that someone else could have done?**

....

☐ **What things happened today that were totally unexpected?**

....

☐ **What did you do today that could have been systemized ...**

On a computer?...

In your diary?..

By talking it out with others?..

By having a daily/weekly work plan?...

☐ **What blocks/barriers did you encounter today that interfered with your goals?**

....

Concluding Thoughts

Effective utilization of time requires examining how your time is spend in relation to the goals/dreams/aspirations you have set yourself.

THE IMPORTANCE OF RELAXATION

Lawrence (1988), Happ (1992) and many others have stressed the importance of personnel having access to relaxation situations in terms of healthy self-esteem, stress management and quality leisure.

We would concur, and argue that if you are to have a self-esteem that is based on a well balanced ideal image, that you need ready access to **relaxation activities**.

Relaxation will also be a vital contribution to your stress management.

We would like to suggest that you could enhance your relaxation status by considering the following suggestions:

Sit comfortably

☐ Ensure all your limbs are limp.

☐ Take off your shoes.

☐ Fix your eyes on a point on the wall or ceiling (do not raise your head).

☐ The moment you experience any discomfort close your eyes.

Now ...

☐ Breathe in, slowly, until you feel this breathing happening automatically.

☐ Focus on the breath you have now in the abdomen ... fill your abdomen with each intake, not just the upper part.

☐ Focus on your stomach muscles ... relax them.

☐ Relax your neck muscles the same way.

☐ Focus now on each part of your body. Begin with your toes and slowly bring your attention upwards.

☐ At this time, bring to your mind a relaxing vista; e.g. a warm, country scene on a still day ... only the call of a bird, the babble of a running river, disturb the silence.

> Now ...
>
> Imagine you can see a small leaf floating in the river.
> Follow its path to the sea ... It will take 5 minutes to get there.
>
> Finally ...
>
> slowly, gently open your eyes.

(It is often a good idea to play suitably relaxing music whilst you undertake the above activity.)

Chapter 5
Making Maximum Use of the Self-Esteem Workbooks

The Importance of Drama/Role-Playing

A student with low self-esteem often has significant anxieties related to performing in front of others, especially their peer group. A 'fear of failure' will prevent students from attempting tasks they might make mistakes with or in attempting new and novel tasks.

Role-playing, especially when it has been well prepared and conducted by someone who the 'at risk' student knows and trusts, can remove the student from their anxieties for a short time and allow them to attempt tasks without a 'fear of failure'. In this situation they will be prepared to take certain acceptable risks..

Mentors should carefully select from these, take on some of the roles themselves and gradually involve their students in this activity.

Establishing quality time

The books have been designed to provide significant others (self-esteem mentors) with opportunities to share quality time and experiences with their children. The success of the activities will largely depend on the quality of the relationship the mentor is able to establish with the child with whom he or she is working.

The clear purpose of this work is to help young people to develop into decent adults, like Nisha, one of the editor's former students who now works in the media in London.

Trust activities

As has been pointed out earlier in this manual, a key component in the mentor/child relationship is **trust**. Children need to feel they are understood, accepted and 'believed in'. We would encourage self-esteem mentors to begin each session by sharing a trust activity with their child/children.

Trust is gained with patience, thoughtfulness and care over a period of time. It can be damaged or lost in a second by careless or inconsiderate behaviour (displayed by a mentor.) Self-esteem mentors need to cultivate and protect the trust that an individual offers and shares. (Karl Rohnke, 1984.)

In our work we stress the importance of encouraging **'acceptable risk taking'** amongst children.

When a group of children develop a feeling of trust, the members begin to think ...

"If I try something and fail in this situation people will support my efforts. When I am in the care of my self-esteem mentor I will not be laughed at or made to appear foolish. Here my ideas and comments will be considered without ridicule.'

If the self-esteem mentor is able to establish trust, his/her children will become risk takers. If they take an acceptable risk and fail, the objective becomes that they learn to modify their risk taking. If they take an acceptable risk and succeed, they build their confidence and enhance their self-trust.

' ... Taking risks stretches your limits ... it makes you more agile, more informed, more sympathetic, more confident and more sure that you are lovable and capable.' (Sydney Simon, 1988)

The following selection of **Trust Games**, sometimes referred to as ice-breakers, are offered to self-esteem mentors. It is suggested that mentors should draw from these to begin each session.

The authors of this manual have used these activities over many years of working in the area of self-esteem. The original sources of these activities are difficult to track down. However, our research suggests that the following sources have cited them. If we have overlooked other significant sources, we offer our apologies.

SOURCES OF GAMES AND ACTIVITIES

Canfield J and Wells H (1976) 100 Ways To Enhance Self Concept in the Classroom. Prentice-Hall, New Jersey

Gram R K and Guest P M (1977) Activities For Developing Positive Self Awareness. Milliken Publishing Co. pp. 103 - 138

Hawley R C and Hawley I L (1975) Developing Human Potential. E.P.A. Press, Massachusetts pp 1-2

Rohnke K (1984) Silver Bullets. Project Adventure, Iowa

Simon S (1988) Getting Unstuck: Breaking Through Your Barriers to Change. Warner, New York

GROUP GAMES

Name Games

❏ The Picnic

Tell the group you are all going on a picnic. Everyone has to say their name and something they will bring. You begin and name something beginning with the same initial as your name, e.g. 'I am Julie and I'm bringing jam.' As each person says what they will bring, you say whether they can come or not, according to whether they have selected something beginning with the same initial as their name. (n.b. Don't tell participants the rule!)

e.g.   "I am Simon and I'm bringing tuna." would be wrong.
           "I am **S**imon and I'm bringing **s**almon." is right.

Progress around the circle until everyone is coming on the picnic or until you think you need to explain the rule of the game because it is frustrating people or taking too long.

❏ The Rhyming Game

One person starts by introducing himself or herself,

e.g.   "I'm Mark, I like playing in the park."
           The next,
           "I'm Sue, I like wearing blue."

Each person says all the rhymes preceding theirs and then adds their own. Continue until all have been introduced.

Energisers

❏ Fruit Bowl

A vigorous exercise, good to get a group moving at any time. Variations can be models of cars, popular 'pop' groups, etc. Everyone is designated either apple, orange or pear. The caller in the middle has no 'name' and no chair. When the caller calls one of the 'names', everyone with that 'name' has to swap places but must not swap with someone next to them. The 'caller' has to try and get a chair. The one left becomes the caller. Sometimes the call can be 'fruit-bowl'. Then everyone changes places.

❏ Someone Who

Instead of using names, call out a description which fits people in the group, e.g. someone who is wearing glasses, has freckles, has long hair, has a birthday in June, is wearing sandshoes, didn't do their homework last night, has a brother (or sister) etc.

❏ The Group Knot

A good warm-up or finishing exercise - fun at any time. Each member takes one hand of two different members who are not standing next to them. This forms a tangle of arms in the centre of the group. No member can hold two hands of one person. Members must then untangle themselves without letting go of hands.

❏ Paper, Scissors, Stone

Members face each other in pairs, both hands behind the back. On an order one hand is brought to the front in one of three positions:

Paper - palm up, hand outstretched

Scissors - hands clenched except for first and middle fingers held outstretched like scissors

Stone - fist clenched

One partner wins as follows:

Scissors - cuts paper   Stone - blunts scissors   Paper - wraps stone

❏ Dead Soldiers

One person watches. Everyone walks around. At a command members lie on the floor as if shot. The first person seen moving becomes the watcher.

❏ Statues

As above, except members move around until on the count of 3 they have to freeze. First person to move, even the smallest move, becomes the watcher.

❏ The Great Escape

Group members, bar one, form a tight circle with their arms tightly locked around each other. The 'prisoner' stands in the centre and tries to escape - either between, over or under the wall. Members must not use hands or arms to prevent the 'prisoner's' escape, just keep themselves firmly locked with their neighbour.

❏ Follow the Action

Members sit in a circle. The leader initiates an action, e.g. clapping, tapping knees, clicking fingers, stamping feet, etc. The rest of the group has to follow the leader's action. One member is kept outside. When the action has started, the 'outsider' comes in and stands in the centre of the circle, trying to guess who the leader is. When they guess, they change places with someone else who goes outside.

❏ Walking the Gauntlet

Two teams face one another. In turn, one member from each team walks down between the teams. The opposing team has to try to and make them laugh. They cannot touch them, only make faces or comments. If the person walking the gauntlet laughs, they join the other team. The game continues until one team has all members.

❏ Running the Gauntlet

Two rows are formed with arms and hands extended in front, with fingers touching. A member runs from some distance at a good speed straight into the 'wall' of arms. The arms must drop, just as the person is about to touch them. A quick and confident runner and split second timing of the 'wall' of arms creates a great 'buzz' for the runner.

❏ Clap-Click

All members sit in a circle. The leader initiates an action, e.g. clapping. The next person repeats it and adds something, for example, clicking. This process is continued with each person in the group adding something, until everyone is too confused or exhausted to continue.

❏ Scissors

A pair of scissors, held open or closed, is passed around the circle, beginning with the leader. One other group member has been told the 'secret'. As they pass the scissors, each person tries to pass it correctly, saying e.g. 'I pass the scissors to Judi open (or closed)', as they try to guess the 'secret'. As the scissors are passed from one to the other the leader pronounces 'right' or 'wrong'. The 'secret' has in fact, nothing to do with the scissors. If the person passing the scissors has their legs or feet crossed, the scissor passing is pronounced 'right', if not the scissor passing is 'wrong'. Gradually members of the group guess 'the secret'. The game continues until all have guessed or until the group's patience is exhausted. Tell the group the 'secret' if it has not been understood by everyone by the time you stop playing.

❏ Pass the Squeeze

This is a gentle, quiet game which develops trust and settles a group. Everybody stands in a circle holding hands. They pass a gentle 'squeeze' around the circle from hand to hand in a clockwise direction very subtly. Members go out in turn, then return to stand in the centre and identify where the 'squeeze' is.

When they do, they change places with the member whom they caught. Keep playing the game until members become very skilled at disguising where the 'squeeze' is.

❏ Paper Stand

See how many can stand on a sheet of newspaper. Then fold it in half and try again. Keep on folding the paper until the members cannot crowd on the paper any longer (even by standing on one toe and grabbing one another for balance). Try it a few times to improve the method.

❏ Back-to-Back Fours

Groups of four sit on the floor, backs together and arms interlocked. They must stand up without using their arms, then run across the room without losing the close contact of their backs pressed together. This game can be started in pairs and numbers can gradually be increased.

❏ Get the Ball

Use a soft ball. Place two lines of chairs facing each other and number off. The leader calls a number and the member from each team runs for the ball to carry it back to their seat. The one who fails to get it tries to tag the other member. If the member succeeds in either case their team gains a point.

❏ Find the Palm

Two players stand at arm's length facing one another. Players raise their arms, touch each other's palms and close their eyes. They then drop arms and turn around three times keeping their eyes closed. Without talking, each tries to locate the other by touching palms again.

❒ Spiral

Members of the group join hands in a circle. One hand is let go and one person leads off in a spiral. The other stands very still and becomes the centre of the spiral until they are 'wrapped up'. Very slowly is best. The central person tries to get out without letting go hands.

❒ Catch the Tail of the Dragon

Grasp one another around the waist, forming a chain. One person becomes the head and one the tail of the dragon. The tail person can 'wear' a tail e.g. a jumper or scarf dangling. The head tries to catch the tail without breaking the 'body' of the dragon.

❒ Ball and String Game *(For use in Group Discussions.)*

For this you need a ball of string or fairly heavy wool. The leader begins by taking the end of the string, then passes the ball to a group member who is speaking or whom they wish to encourage to say something. It is then passed in turn to different members of the group as they join in discussion or are encouraged to do so because someone gives them the ball. When they have finished speaking, they immediately hand it on. It can be used to tell a 'group story' or when a general discussion is taking place.

This is a good game to encourage quiet members and also to stop interruption and dominations by one member if a group is having a heated discussion. Members cannot speak unless they have the ball (including the leader).

The visual pattern created by the string gives a real sense of group cohesion and indicates individuals' contributions to the discussion. Ask members to say how they feel about the game after they have played it. They might find it awkward at first, but with practice, they can become quite adept. It is a useful way of developing group unity and equality.

❒ Pass the Paper *(Affirming one another.)*

Group members are given an A4 sized piece of paper. They write their names on top and pass it to the group member on their left. The person on the left writes a positive comment about the person whose name is on the sheet of paper, then folds the paper upward to cover what they have written. They then pass it to the person on their left who in turn writes a positive comment and folds it upwards. This is repeated all around the group till the paper is returned to the owner.

Only positive things should be written - otherwise pass. Group members can read the comments aloud or privately as they wish.

CONFLICT RESOLUTION

It would be naive to think that a self-esteem mentor working with a group of children will not be confronted with conflict situations.

❐ Two children hotly disputing their 'rights' in a particular situation.

❐ A child disputing a requirement set by the mentor.

Conflict has the potential to ...

❐ destroy trust;

❐ shake an individual's confidence;

❐ destroy acceptable risk taking.

Thus we advocate that to make maximum use of the self-esteem books a self-esteem mentor needs access to an appropriate conflict resolution strategy. In light of this, we offer the following general considerations and specific strategies.

General Considerations For Self-Esteem Mentors

When confronted with a conflict between children, mentors should consider the following suggestions ...

❐ Focus on the behaviour displayed, not the personality of the individuals involved.

❐ Mentors need to recognize the conflict as a mutual problem solving situation.

❐ Mentors need to recognise that all protagonists involved in the conflict identify and communicate the feelings they have related to the conflict.

❐ Mentors need to emphasize to participants that they may well need to be prepared to accept that they are wrong. As mediators, mentors also need to be prepared to accept that their initial interpretation of the conflict may have been wrong.

❐ Mentors need to become particularly astute in recognizing the non-verbal messages being displayed by the conflict participants.

❐ The most important skill a mentor needs to bring to a conflict situation is reflective listening.

A Specific Strategy Worthy Of Consideration - Based On Rational Emotional Therapy

☐ **A: Define the Problem Area**

Write down your perception of the parameters of the conflict.

> e.g. Frank reacts aggressively to every task I set. He claims ... "it's a waste of time, stupid". He often attempts to impose his views on other members of the group.

☐ **B: Identify your Emotional Response to the Conflict**

e.g. When Frank does this ...

I feel intimidated.
I feel angry.
I feel frustrated.

☐ **C: Use Self Talk**

Talk out loud to yourself the scenario associated with the conflict.

> e.g. Frank is experiencing a great deal of academic difficulty at school. He has a long history of failure at school. He is often put down by his peers for his poor academic performance. I really quite like Frank. I think a great deal of this inappropriate behaviour is directed at avoiding failing in front of the group and me.

☐ **D: Identify the Behaviours Displayed During the Conflict**

> e.g. Frank avoids eye contact. He will often swear. Sometimes he refuses to respond at all. He often puts group members down. I tend to be very defensive .. saying 'yes' when I don't mean it.

Increasingly I am avoiding contact with him.

☐ **E: Identify Possible Solutions/Strategies**
- a) I need to organize for some quality time with Frank.
- b) I need to share some of my failures with him.
- c) I need to provide my group with some 'failure free' activities.
- d) I need to provide positive feedback towards Frank's relative strengths.

☐ **F: Reflect on Possible Outcomes**
- a) What would be the worst outcome of this conflict?
- b) What would be the most successful outcome of this conflict?

If a self-esteem mentor encourages direct conflict with a student he/she is working with or observes this occurring between students in the group then:

☐ Introduce students to the above strategy.

☐ Relate 'conflict situations' you have experienced.

☐ Direct students to one or more of the conflict resolution activities included in Books 2 or 3.

☐ Use humour to defuse some of the accompanying emotional tension.

MANAGING THE CHILDREN'S BEHAVIOUR

Whilst a trusting, empathized, caring relationship has been advocated in this programme, it is recognized that self-esteem mentors have a need to positively manage children's behaviours. To this end we offer the following suggestions.

KEY CONSIDERATIONS

1. In managing children's behaviour the old adage that prevention is better than cure is most appropriate. This requires mentors to quickly establish clearly defined **behavioural boundaries**. To do this mentors need to:

   ☐ Display a firm, confident, pleasant, interested and enthusiastic manner with the children during your initial contact.

   ☐ Make your expectations about required behaviour clear to children. Keep your voice controlled and modulated. An air of firmness and self assurance will help you to win a child's respect.

   ☐ Limit your directions to those that are absolutely necessary - say 2 or 3 at a time, to ensure that effective directions are issued.

   Your behavioural boundaries should be determined by standards/values that are important to you.

2. Group rules will contribute to **effective behavioural boundaries**. A group discussion should be held during your initial session in which group members should reach consensus on approximately four rules that will apply exclusively to their group. These should be recorded and then distributed to each group member.

3. There are a number of control techniques that will assist mentors to manage children's behaviour. These include:

   ☐ For minor problems such as inattention or inappropriate conversation between children, **non-verbal techniques** such as a pause or a look in the direction of the offender can often solve the difficulty without stopping your activity.

   ☐ **Presence:** This involves the mentor moving over to where a minor disturbance in the group is taking place. Generally, this will result in a quietening down of the situation.

   ☐ **Rebuke:** A rebuke may be effective in resolving an individual or group disruption. However mentors need to use this with caution. In some cases of attention-seeking behaviour the rebuke can be counter-productive. In using rebuke the mentor might find the following procedures helpful:

   − With a quiet but authoritative voice name the pupil, issue a mild rebuke and phrase it in such as way as to related it to the task in hand. e.g. *"John, you won't get your camp food order completed if you continue to annoy Mary!"*

   − Pause, and follow up the rebuke with a sustained look at John. Praise someone else who is on task.

   ☐ **Separation:** This involves removing the child from the immediate area for a short period of time. Before doing this you should give the student one quiet warning.- *"John, if you do not pay attention, I will have to move you away from the group."*

Move him to another desk, or open space within the room **but not outside the room**.

❑ **Praise (affirmation):** When you give praise make sure that it has been earned through genuine achievement. When giving praise be simple, direct and sincere. Also use non-verbal language such as a smile or a gesture to reinforce your pleasure at the achievement.

❑ **Punishment:** Mentors should endeavour to avoid punishing children. In the main if a mentor concludes that punishment is warranted the matter should be referred to the programme co-ordinator or child's teacher.

If it is decided that punishment is required than punishment should be:

– used as a last resort and only in response to repeated misbehaviour;

– based on one warning;

– immediate;

– directly related to the offence;

– fair and consistent - but firm enough to stop the misbehaviour;

– used in conjunction with other techniques, such as discussion, to strengthen an acceptable response.

REFERENCES

Bandura, A. (1977a). *Social learning theory.* Englewood Cliffs, NJ: Prentice-Hall.

Bandura, A. (1977b). Self-efficacy: Toward a unifying theory of behavioural change. *Psychological Review*, 84, 191-215.

Bandura, A. (1982). Self-efficacy mechanism in human agency. *American Psychologist*, 37, 122-147.

Bandura, A. (1983). Self-evaluative and self-efficiency mechanisms governing the motivational effects of goal systems. *Journal of Personality and Social Psychology,* 38, 1017-1028.

Bandura, A. (1986). *Social foundations of thought and action: A special cognitive theory.* Englewood Cliffs, NJ: Prentice-Hall.

Bandura, A. (1988). Perceived self-efficacy: Exercise of control through self-belief. In J.P. Dauwalker, M. Perrez, & V. Hobbi (Eds.), *Annual series of European research in behaviour therapy* (Vol 2, pp. 27 - 59). Lisse, Netherlands: Swets & Zeitlinger.

Bandura, A. (1989a). Social cognitive theory. In R. Vasta (Ed.), *Annuals of child development* (Vol 6, pp 1-60). Greenwich, CT: JAI Press.

Bandura, A. (1989b). Human agency in social cognitive theory. *American Psychologist*, 44 (9), 1175-1184.

Bandura, A & Wood, R.E. (1989). Effect of perceived controllability and performance standards on self-regulation of complex decision-making. *Journal of Personality and Social Psychology*, 56, 805-814.

Bardwell, R. (1981). Feedback: How does it function? *Journal of Experimental Education*, 50, 4-9.

Bednar, R., Wells, M., & Peterson, S. (1989). *Self-esteem: Paradoxes and innovations in clinical theory and practice.* Washington, D.C.: American Psychological Association.

Berne, E. (1964). *Games people play: The psychology of human relationships.* London: Penguin.

Berne, E. (1972). *What do you say after hello? The psychology of human destiny.* NY: Grove Press.

Brown, J.D., Collins, R.L., & Schmidt, G.W. (1988). Self-esteem and direct versus indirect forms of self-enhancement. *Journal of Personality and Social Psychology*, 55, 445-453.

Burns, R.B. (1979). *The self-concept in theory, measurement, development and behavior.* NY: Longmans.

Burns, R.B. (1982). *Self-concept development and education.* Sydney, Australia: Holt, Rinehart & Winston.

Byrne, B.M. (1984). The general/academic self-concept nomological network: A review of construct validation research. *Review of Educational Research*, 54, 427-456.

Cannella, G.S. (1986). Praise and concrete rewards: concerns for childhood education. *Childhood Education*, 62 (4), 297-301.

Chapman, J.W., Lambourne, R., & Silva, P.A. (1990). Some antecedents of academic self-concept: A longitudinal study. *British Journal of Educational Psychology*, 60, 142-152.

Clems, H., & Bean, R. (1981). *Self-Esteem: The key to your child's well being.* NY: Putnam's.

Coopersmith, S. (1981). *The antecedents of self-esteem.* Palo Alto, CA: Consulting Psychologists Press. (Original work published 1967).

Coopersmith, S., & Feldman, R. (1974). Fostering a positive self-concept and high self-esteem in the classroom. In R.H. Coop & K. White (Eds.), *Psychological concepts in the classroom* (chapter 7). NY: Harper & Row.

Covington, M.V. (1984). The self worth, theory of achievement motivation: Findings and implications. *The Elementary School Journal*, 85 (1), 5-20.

Dittes, J.E. (1959). Attractiveness of group of a function of self-esteem and acceptance by group. *Journal of Abnormal and Social Psychology*, 59, 77-82.

Doherty, J. (1980). An exploratory investigation into the relationship between self-esteem and teaching performance in a group of student teachers. *Educational Review*, 32 (1), 21-35.

Epstein, S. (1973, May). The self-concept revisited: Or a theory of a theory. *American Psychologist*, pp. 404-416.

Erikson, E.H. (1959). Identity and the life cycle. *Psychological Issues*, 1, 1-171.

Erikson, E.H. (1968). Identity: *Youth and crisis.* NY: Norton.

Fitts, W.H. (1981). Issues regarding self-concept change. In M.D. Lynch, A.A. Norem-Hebeisen & K. Gergen (Eds.), *Self-concept: Advances in theory and research* (pp. 261-272). Cambridge, MA: Ballinger.

Friedenberg, W., & Gillis, J. (1977). An experimental study of the effectiveness of attitude change techniques for enhancing self-esteem. *Journal of Clinical Psychology*, 33 (4), 1120-1124.

Gurney, P. (1986). Self-esteem in the classroom: Theoretical perspectives and assessment issues. *School Psychology International*, 7, 199-209.

Hansford, B.C., & Hattie, J.A. (1982). The relationship between self and achievement/performance measures. *Review of Educational Research*, 52 (1), pp. 123-142.

Harter, S. (1983). Development perspectives on the self-system. In E.M. Hetheringon (Ed.), *Handbook of Child Psychology: Vol 4. Socialization, personality, and social development* (4th ed., pp. 275-385). NY: Wiley.

Harter, S. (1988). The construction and conservation of the self: James and Cooley revisited. In D.K. Lapsley & F.C. Power (Eds.), *Self, ego, and identity: integrative approaches* (pp42-70). NY: Springer-Verlag.

Hattie, J. (1992). *Self concept.* Hillsdale, N.J. Lawrence Erlbaum.

Hattie, J. (1991). *Processes of integration of self-concept.* Paper presented at the Annual Conference of the Australian Association for Educational Research, Gold Coast, Queensland, Australia.

Hattie, J.A. & Hansford, B.C. (1983). Reading performance and self-assessment: What is the relationship? *Reading Education*, 8, 17-23.

Jersild, A.T. (1952). *In search of self: An exploration of the role of the school in promoting self-understanding.* NY: Columbia University Teachers College.

Kaplan, H.B. (1975). The self-esteem motive. In H.B. Kaplan (Ed.), *Self-attitudes and deviant behaviour* (pp. 10-31). Pacific Palisades, CA: Goodyear.

LaBenne, W.D., & Green, B.I. (1969). *Educational implications of self-concept theory.* Pacific Palisades, California: Goodyear.

Laing, R.D. (1969). *Self and others.* NY: Pantheon Books.

Lawrence, D. (1985). Improving self-esteem and reading. *Educational Research*, 27 (3), 194-200.

Lawrence, D. (1988). *Enhancing self-esteem in the classroom.* London: Paul Chapman.

Leahy, R.L. (Ed.). (1985). *The development of the self.* NY: Academic Press.

Markus, H., & Wurf, E.. (1987). The dynamic self-concept: A social psychological perspective. *Annual Review of Psychology*, 38, 299-337.

Marsh, H.W. (1990a) The structure of academic self-concept: The Marsh/Shavelson model. *Journal of Educational Psychology*, 82 (4), 623-636.

Marsh, H.W., Barnes, J., Carins, L., & Tidman, M. (1984). Self-description questionnaire: Age and sex effects in the structure and level of self-concept for pre-adolescent children. *Journal of Educational Psychology*, 76, 940-956.

Marsh, H.W., Richards, G.E., & Barnes, J. (1986). Multidimensional self-concept: A long term follow up of the effect of participation in an Outward Bound program. *Personality and Social Psychology Bulletin*, 20, 509-528.

Marsh, H.W. & Shavelson, R. (1985). Self-concept: Its multifaceted, hierarchical structure. *Educational Psychologist*, 20, 107-125.

Marshall, H.H. (1989). Research in review: The development of self-concept. *Young Children*, 44 (5), 44-49.

Offer, D., Ostrov, E., & Howard, K.I. (1977). The self-image of adolescents: A study of four cultures. *Journal of Youth and Adolescence*, 6, 265-280.

Purkey, W.W. (1968). The search for self: Evaluating student self concepts, *Research Bulletin*, 4 (2), 1-31.

Purkey, W.W. (1970). *Self concept and school achievement.* Englewood Cliffs, NJ: Prentice-Hall.

Purkey, W.W., & Novak, J. (1984). *Inviting school success: A self concept approach to teaching and learning* (2nd ed.). Belmont, CA: Wadsworth.

Renshaw, p. (1990). Self-esteem research and equity programs for girls: A reassessment. In J. Kenway & S. Wills (Eds.), *Hearts and minds: Self-esteem and the schooling of girls.* Australia: The Falmer Press.

Rogers, C.R. (1950). The significance of the self-regarding attitudes and perceptions. In M.L. Reymert (Ed.), *The Mooseheart Symposium* (pp. 374-382). NY: McGraw-Hill.

Rogers, C.R. (1951). *Client-centred therapy: Its current practice, implications, and theory.* Boston: Houghton-Mifflin.

Rogers, C.R. (1961). *On becoming a person.* Boston: Houghton-Mifflin.

Rogers, C.R. (1963). Learning to be free. *National Education Association Journal*, 52, 28-30.

Rosenberg, M. (1979). *Conceiving the self.* NY: Basic.

Sarbin, T.R., & Resenberg, B.G. (1955). Contributions to role-taking theory: IV. A method for obtaining a qualitive estimate of the self. *The Journal of Social Psychology*, 42, 71-81.

Schillling, D. (1986). Self-esteem: concerns, strategies, resources. *Academic Therapy*, 21 (3), 301-307.

Shavelson, R.J., & Bolus, R. (1982). Self-concept: The interplay of theory and methods. *Journal of Educational Psychology*, 74, 3-17.

Shavelson, R.J., & Marsh, H.W. (1986) On the structure on self-concept. In R. Schwarzer (Ed.), *Anxiety and cognition* (pp. 305-330) Hillsdale, NJ: Lawrence Erlbaum Associates.

Smith I.D. (1982). The development of children's self-concept: An important educational aim. *Leader*, 2, 19-22.

Song, I.S., & Hattie, J. (1984). Home environment, self-concept, and academic achievement: A casual modelling approach. *Journal of Educational Psychology*, 76, 1269-1281.

Song, I.S., & Hattie, J. (1985). Relationships between self-concept and achievement. *Journal of Research in Personality*, 19, 365-372.

Stanton, H.E. (1980). The modification of student self-concept. *Studies in Higher Education*, 5 (1) 71-76.

Wells, L.E., & Marwell, G. (1976). *Self-esteem: Its conceptualizing and measurement.* Beverly Hills: Sagel

Wylie, R.C. (1974). *The self-concept: A review of methodological considerations and measuring instruments.* Lincoln, NE: University of Nebraska Press.

Wylie, R.C. (1979). *The self-concept.* Lincoln, NE.: University of Nebraska Press.

Wylie, R.C. (1989). *Measures of self-concept.* Lincoln, NE.: University of Nebraska Press.

Yawkey, T.D. (Ed.). (1980). *The self concept of the young child.* Provo, Utah: Brigham Young University Press.

Supporting

Literacy *and*

Numeracy

A Guide for Learning Support Assistants

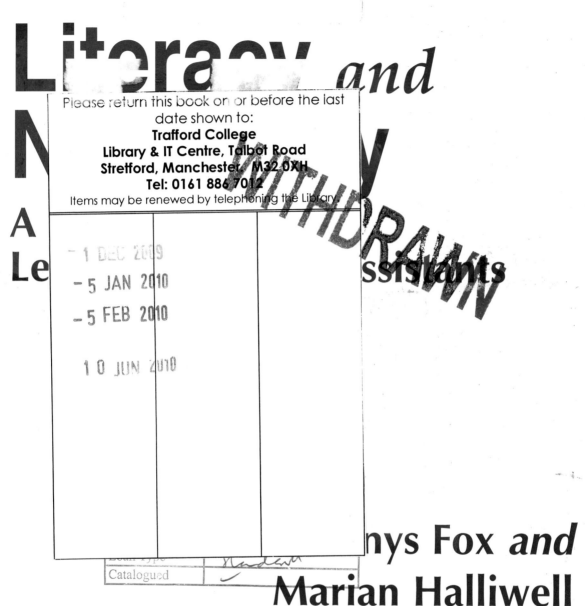

Glenys Fox *and* Marian Halliwell

David Fulton Publishers

London

David Fulton Publishers Ltd,
414 Chiswick High Road, London W4 5TF

www.fultonpublishers.co.uk

First published in Great Britain by David Fulton Publishers 2000
Reprinted 2000, 2001 (twice), 2003
10 9 8 7 6 5

British Library Cataloguing in Publication Data

A catalogue record for this book is available from the British Library.

ISBN 1–85346–679–4

Typeset by FiSH Books, London
Printed and bound in Great Britain by Ashford Colour Press Limited, Gosport, Hants